SLIM GOODBODY'S NUTRITION EDITION

Vital Vegetables

CRABTREE
Publishing Company
www.crabtreebooks.com

Crabtree Publishing Company
www.crabtreebooks.com

Series development, writing, and packaging:
John Burstein, Slim Goodbody Corp.

Editors:
Molly Aloian
Reagan Miller
Mark Sachner, Water Buffalo Books

Editorial director:
Kathy Middleton

Production coordinator:
Kenneth Wright

Prepress technician:
Kenneth Wright

Designer:
Tammy West, Westgraphix LLC

Photos:
Chris Pinchback, Pinchback Photography

Photo credits:
© Slim Goodbody, iStockphotos, and Shutterstock images.

"Slim Goodbody" and Pinchback photos, copyright,
© Slim Goodbody

Acknowledgements:
The author would like to thank the following people for
their help in this project:
Christine Burstein, Olivia Davis, Kylie Fong, Nathan
Levig, Havana Lyman, Andrew McBride, Lulu McClure,
Ben McGinnis, Esme Power, Joe Ryan

"Slim Goodbody" and "Slim Goodbody's Nutrition Edition"
are registered trademarks of the Slim Goodbody Corp.

Library and Archives Canada Cataloguing in Publication

Burstein, John
    Vital vegetables / John Burstein.

(Slim Goodbody's nutrition edition)
Includes index.
ISBN 978-0-7787-5045-1 (bound).--ISBN 978-0-7787-5060-4 (pbk.)

    1. Vegetables in human nutrition--Juvenile literature. 2. Nutrition--
Juvenile literature. I. Title. II. Series:°Burstein, John. Slim Goodbody's
nutrition edition.

QP144.V44B87 2010   j641.3'5   C2009-903880-3

Library of Congress Cataloging-in-Publication Data

Burstein, John.
    Vital vegetables / John Burstein.
        p. cm. -- (Slim Goodbody's nutrition edition)
    Includes index.
    ISBN 978-0-7787-5060-4 (pbk. : alk. paper) -- ISBN 978-0-7787-5045-1 (rein-
forced library binding : alk. paper)
    1. Vegetables in human nutrition--Juvenile literature. 2. Nutrition--Juvenile
literature. 3. Children--Nutrition--Requirements--Juvenile literature. I. Title.
II. Series.

QP144.V44B87 2010
613.2--dc22

2009024754

Crabtree Publishing Company

Published in Canada
Crabtree Publishing
616 Welland Ave.
St. Catharines, Ontario
L2M 5V6

Published in the United States
Crabtree Publishing
PMB16A
350 Fifth Ave., Suite 3308
New York, NY 10118

Published in the United Kingdom
Crabtree Publishing
White Cross Mills
High Town, Lancaster
LA1 4XS

Published in Australia
Crabtree Publishing
386 Mt. Alexander Rd.
Ascot Vale (Melbourne)
VIC 3032

CONTENTS

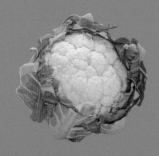
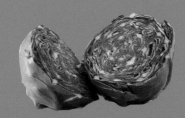

GREETINGS

My name is Slim Goodbody.
I want to ask you two questions.

1. Do you want to be healthy?
I hope you said **YES**.

2. If you do not eat right,
can you be healthy?
I hope you said **NO**.

The U.S. food pyramid helps you eat right.

There are six stripes on the U.S. food pyramid.

The stripes stand for the five different food groups plus oils.

GRAINS
VEGETABLES
FRUITS
OILS
MILK
MEAT
& BEANS

This book is about the vegetable food group.

VEGETABLES!

Vegetables belong on the green stripe in the U.S. food pyramid. Vegetables come in many colors.

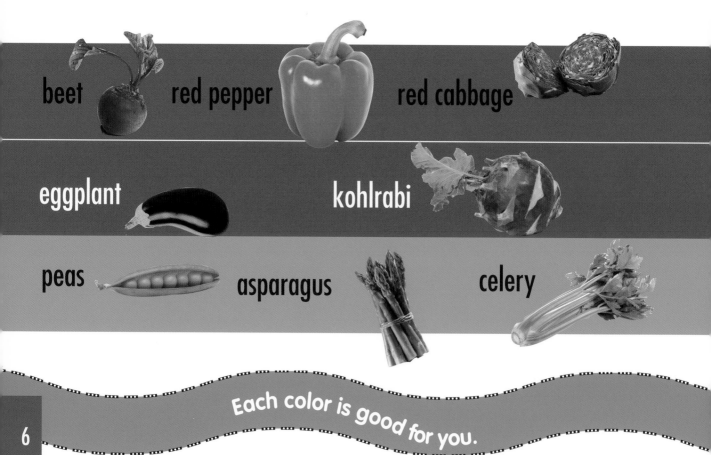

beet

red pepper

red cabbage

eggplant

kohlrabi

peas

asparagus

celery

Each color is good for you.

 spinach

 collard green

carrot

pumpkin

sweet potatoes

bell pepper

butternut squash

onion

cauliflower

potatoes

All Vegetables are Plants

Different kinds of vegetables come from different parts of plants.

We eat the leaves.

We eat the stems.

To stay healthy, eat vegetables every day.

We eat the seeds.

We eat the flower.

We eat the stalks.

We eat the bulbs.

We eat the roots.

We eat the tubers.

AROUND THE WORLD

NORTH AMERICA

sweet corn

sweet potatoes

yams

squash

SOUTH AMERICA

Vegetables grow all around the world.

10

kale

beets

eggplant

ASIA

EUROPE

AFRICA

cucumbers

rhubarb

AUSTRALIA

okra

gourds

The same kind of vegetable can even grow in many places.

GROW YOUR OWN

Growing your own vegetables is fun.

Growing veggies is not hard.
You can grow them in your yard.

And in cities, you can still
Grow veggies on your windowsill.

Growing your own veggies helps the Earth.

To get started, all you need
Is a little dirt and a little seed.

Plant the seed and water well.
In its hole, the seed will swell.

As sunshine warms the ground above,
The seed feels Mother Nature's love.

A shoot appears and starts to grow
Upward from its home below.

And suddenly, the shoot pops through
As if to say, "Good day to you!"

BIG, BIG, BIG!

Some people can grow their own vegetables very big.

Big vegetables
still come from
small seeds.

Have you ever seen such a big vegetable?

VEGETABLES HELP YOUR BODY

Vegetables do good things for your body.

Vegetables have a lot of vitamins and minerals.

Some vegetables help keep your skin soft.

Some vegetables help keep your teeth hard.

Some vegetables help keep your heart strong.

Some vegetables keep your brain smart.

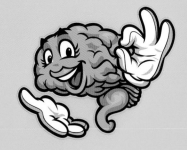

Some vegetables help cuts heal.

Some vegetables help your body fight germs.

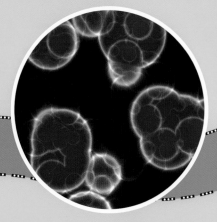

VEGETABLES YOU NEED EACH DAY

You need 1 ½ cups (375 ml) of vegetables every day.

Feel free to mix and match any way you like.

You can use these two lists to help you get the vegetables you need. Each day, eat something from the ONE CUP LIST and something from the ½ CUP LIST.

ONE CUP LIST

12 baby carrots
1 large bell pepper
1 large sweet potato
1 cup of cooked spinach
1 medium baked potato
3 medium spears of broccoli
1 cup of vegetable juice
1 cup of cooked
    bean sprouts

1/2 CUP LIST

6 baby carrots
1 stalk of celery
5 broccoli florets
½ acorn squash
1 cup of raw green lettuce
1 palm-sized piece of tofu
½ cup of vegetable juice
1 small pepper

Try to eat some raw veggies each day.

ANY TIME

Almost
any time is
a good time
to eat vegetables.

You can drink a glass of carrot juice at breakfast.

You can have a salad for lunch.

You can snack on some celery after school.

You can have vegetable soup with dinner.

Order pizza with a veggie topping when you go out.

WORLD FOOD GUIDES

The food pyramid is only one guide to eating well.

To learn more about Canada's Food Guide, check out the web site below.

http://www.nms.on.ca/Elementary/canada.htm

People from different parts of the world often eat different kinds of foods. People use different food guides to help them eat wisely.

THE AUSTRALIAN GUIDE TO HEALTHY EATING

Enjoy a variety of foods every day

Vegetables, legumes

LENTILS
SOYA BEANS
PEAS
CHICKPEAS
CORN

Fruit

ROLLED OATS

MILK
MILK

Milk, yoghurt, cheese

LENTILS

Bread, cereals, rice, pasta, noodles

Lean meat, fish, poultry, eggs, nuts, legumes

Drink plenty of water

Choose these sometimes or in small amounts

BISCUITS

Every day, everyone, everywhere needs vegetables.

WORDS TO KNOW

 **broccoli florets**

 **collard green**

 **eggplant**

 **kohlrabi**

 **shoot**

 **tubers**

FIND OUT MORE

Books

My Food Pyramid, DK Publishing.

Growing Vegetable Soup, Lois Ehlert, Voyager Books.

Web Sites

MyPyramid.gov
http://www.mypyramid.gov/kids/index.html

Slim Goodbody
www.slimgoodbody.com

Printed in the U.S.A.-CG